BASIL OF THE BATTS

The Autobiography of an Aristocratic Dachshund

told by **BAS**
written and expurgated by
JEAN BARBARA BANCROFT

Illustrations by Matthew Frankland

Highgate Publications (Beverley) Limited, 1993

PREFACE

I had originally intended to produce a book of captions and cartoons which would illustrate Basil's personality, following an inspired remark by my friend, Lorraine Kirby, several years ago. Somehow it turned into an autobiography instead.

Writing it has kept Basil very much alive to me and I hope that his distinctive personality will give as much pleasure to readers as it did to me and to others who knew him for the ten years that he did his best to rule my life.

J.B.B.

Published by
Highgate Publications (Beverley) Ltd., 24 Wylies Road, Beverley, HU17 7AP
Telephone (0482) 866826

Printed by
Colourspec, Unit 7, Tokenspire Park, Hull Road, Woodmansey, Beverley, HU17 0TB
Telephone (0482) 864264

ISBN 0 948929 68 5

When I sent Mum the manuscript she said it needed a **Dedication**; I thought I'd dedicated a lot of time and energy to it, but apparently this is a different kind of dedication — so here goes:

To her cousin MARGARET, who really prefers cats, especially Charlie, but who has always given Mum lots of love and encouragement,

also

to all DACHSIE-LOVERS everywhere, to all who love dogs whatever the breed (even Heinz Baked Beans ones) and who know that, after all, 'we **are** only human.'

THANK YOU TO

AUNTIE JANE HODGSON for lending Mum her electric typewriter, and also for helping her, along with UNCLE DUNCAN and AUNTIE TINA, to work out how to use a word processor (because Mum, despite being intelligent because she's a teacher, was totally foxed by it — though what foxes had to do with it, I don't know).

AUNTIE GILL LARKMAN for drawing a much better map of Richmond than Mum was able to do.

UNCLE MATTHEW for his co-operation and AUNTIE CAROLINE for finding him.

AUNTIE JOAN ORAM who had me for holidays and who took me off Mum's hands one week when she was **exhausted.**

AUNTIE PAULINE and UNCLE NIGEL DURIE who had me to stay once when Auntie Joan couldn't have me, and who had to cope with a Battle-of-Wills.

AUNTIE SUE LAWRENCE who looked after me whilst Mum was teaching and who had me to stay once when Mum had an operation (not for 'you know what'!)

AUNTIE SUE and those of Mum's FORMER COLLEAGUES who were so sorry for her when Tickey died that they bought me for her as a consolation. (I hope I was able to make up for Tickey a little bit.)

MISTER EDDIE SIMPSON who cured my panic-attacks and who has some very **A1 Kennels** near Catterick Bridge.

THE PUBLISHERS for being trusting.

LINDA and BILL, my new owners, who took me in when I couldn't manage Mum's stairs any longer and who have given me such a good home (with lots of care and attention) and with whom I am very happy. Mum is very grateful to them for writing letters to her and sending photographs (which show how aristocratic-looking I am.)

GRATIA! (That's Latin for 'Thank you'.)

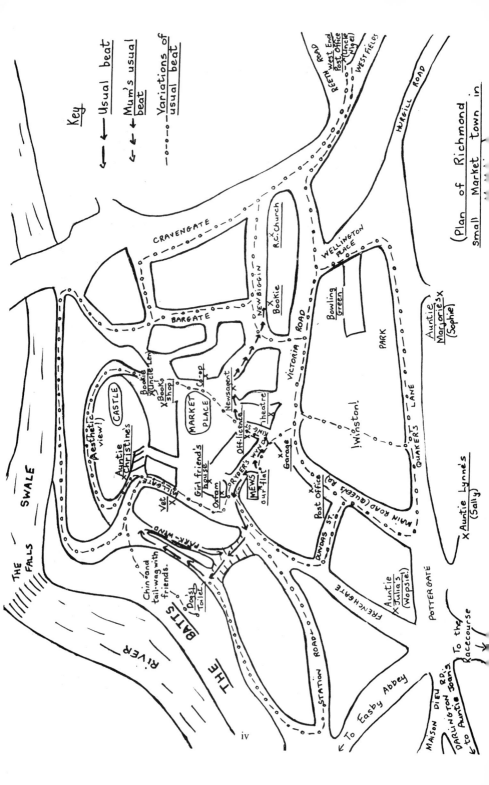

(Plan of Richmond small Market town in ...)

iv

Chapter One

I was born in Scotland and brought up in Yorkshire — but I'm German really; Dachshunds are, aren't they? People who are not polite call me a German sausage but I ignore them; I'm good at doing that.

I don't know who thought up my name, Basil. It's always been good for a laugh though, and I think it sounds aristocratic, in keeping with my nature; I'm a very aristocratic dog and I even have a Roman nose to prove it. My name has always been a good conversation piece. 'Whom is he called after?' people would ask; 'Basil Brush, Basil Hume or Basil Fawlty?' Mum didn't know, as she didn't christen me, but all three would have been appropriate: I have a beautiful brush-like tail; I was brought up a Roman Catholic (though I hated being dragged into church) and with my aristocratic nature I would certainly have fitted in well at Fawlty Towers and I can match Basil Fawlty in disdainfulness (though of course I'm not as rude as he is).

My name used to embarrass Mum when she first got me; I used to embarrass her a lot in fact, one way and another, but she learnt to put a good face on it and in any case she has done her fair share of embarrassing me. Talk about odd! I sometimes had to pretend I didn't belong to her because she really did show me up on occasions.

However, to go back to the beginning . . .

Soon after I was born I came to live in Yorkshire among a lot of other dogs, mostly Dachsies and Dalmatians. We lived outside in kennels owned by two Maiden-Ladies, a long way from nowhere, and we all got on together famously.

When I was a year old, some people came to take me away; they wanted to buy a dog and thought I might do (might do, I ask you!) But that didn't last long because I was back with my friends at the kennels before the day was out. My would-be owners didn't like me. I'm not surprised. I hadn't wanted to go with them in the first place and I let them know in no uncertain terms. They complained that I wouldn't walk on a lead (whatever that was — I'd never seen one before; besides, I wasn't going to go where they wanted!) and they said I wasn't affectionate. I ask you, how can you be affectionate to someone you've never seen before, who takes you away from your friends and tries to drag you around on a long strap attached to a horrible bit of leather fastened round your aristocratic neck? They obviously didn't understand that a dog with my pedigree needs to be treated with a little more respect!

Well, you can imagine how I felt a few weeks later, just before Christmas, when along came somebody else. She was a Maiden-Lady, had white hair (perhaps because it was snowing) and wore two pieces of glass on her face (called spectacles). She looked quite nice but I wasn't going to be fooled again into being adopted and dragged around so I went away and hid. They soon found me though, and I was firmly picked up and dumped in the back of her car where I lay in sullen silence, hoping that no-one was going to start mooning over me and expecting to be licked and made a fuss of. I'll show her right from the start, I decided, that I'm not that kind of dog! I certainly wasn't going to be ingratiating, especially as I didn't want to go to a new home, anyway. However, it soon became obvious that this time things were going to be different.

After we had gone some way, the car stopped and the lady who was with my new owner got out, went into a building and came out with something wrapped in newspaper. Fish-and-Chips! Imagine my surprise when she opened the back of the car and gave the fish to me! I can tell you, it tasted good. Before you could say 'Basil Brush' I had wolfed the lot and for the rest of the journey I had a good think. What I thought was: I might be on to a good thing after all. So I decided that even though it would be beyond my dignity to be actively co-operative at least I wouldn't actually be unco-operative, because there might be more good things to come.

I was right! We dropped off the other lady, called Auntie Sue, and

'I wolfed the lot, and for the rest of the journey I had a good think.'

arrived at my new mum's house. She made a drink and put some rolls-and-paté on a table just high enough for me to reach; I downed the rolls-and-paté and then tried the mug-of-tea. That taught me a lesson; I burnt my tongue! Mum explained that the tea and rolls had been meant for her, not for me, but she laughed and said it was her own fault and so I decided that perhaps she might be **all right**. What is more, she didn't start to drag me around on a lead but let me go to sleep by something warm called a fire; she didn't expect me to show affection either — in fact she virtually ignored me, let me find my feet as it were, and it certainly looked as though I had fallen on my paws, all four of them. I decided to stay.

Chapter Two

At first I slept in a nice warm bed in the hall. Mum would disappear up something called 'stairs' and I wouldn't see her again until morning. Soon, however, I began to feel a bit lonely so I decided one night to go and look for her. It took me a long time to get up those stairs (it's not easy when you're a long dog) but I managed it and found her fast asleep.

I woke her up gently (I'm a very gentle dog, a gentleman in fact — that is part of my aristocratic nature, not like that scruffy animal I used to meet sometimes on my walks, who was very rude and aggressive). Mum seemed quite pleased that I had been so adventurous, but she told me that although I could stay upstairs for the rest of that night it was not to be a precedent. We'll see about that, I thought sleepily, as I settled

'We'll see about that . . .'

3

down on the floor by her bed.

The next day we went for a walk in the snow and my strategy was decided upon; I would let her put me on the lead for a short time (just to get used to it, she said) and so lull her into thinking she was top-dog and then I would begin to show her who was really the boss when it came to where I should sleep.

It didn't take long. By the end of the week I was walking nicely to the lead, and Mum was carrying my basket to her bedroom each night! The art of relating, as everyone knows, is to give and take and end up with a win situation on both sides; I learnt that at the kennels among my friends, but some humans don't seem to understand that; they think that one person has to win and the other, usually the poor dog, has to lose and be submissive. Fortunately Mum understood psychology, especially Dachsie psychology; she specialised in it because my predecessor had been a smooth-haired Dachshund called Tickey, after a threepenny bit, (an unaristocratic name, but he had been born in Africa so I suppose anything goes, there).

I used to get a bit tired of hearing about Tickey. Mum was always telling me how he used to like playing games and what a great sense-of-humour he had. I took no notice. I had heard that my predecessor had been a jealous dog. Now I am not at all jealous by nature, in fact Mum has always said that was one of my **attributes** and that it made her life a lot easier.

Chapter Three

Not long after my arrival we had an **intruder**. I thought he was an intruder, anyway. The front-door bell rang and in walked a Man! I had not seen a man before (except the one who first tried to take me away from the kennels) and I barked at him furiously. Mum didn't seem pleased about this and she let the man into the sitting-room and apologised for my bad manners. I ask you!

I sat and sulked for a while, and that was the beginning of my long-standing suspicion of men. I wasn't all that keen on humans, anyway — I much prefer animals, especially other dogs (I like cats too but they won't play with me, however much I wag my tail) — but Mum was understanding and never tried to force me to be anything other than just polite. Thank goodness she didn't try to make me be affectionate. She was very pleased, though, the day I gave her a quick lick on the nose! She gave me a hug and a kiss back — and that was the beginning of our good relationship. We became very fond of each other without being sloppy; Mum said she didn't care so much for sloppy or subservient dogs, which was why she preferred Dachsies. Very sensible.

She wasn't sensible when it came to Christmas Day though, not long after my arrival. She had to go out and so she left me with a special treat of Turkey. My goodness, it was delicious — but it gave me the Runs. When she came back she had to do some mopping up! On Boxing Day I really embarrassed her; I had the Runs on her friends' white hearthrug. 'Bring Basil with you,' they had said (Mum hadn't wanted to leave me by myself for two days running) and so I went out for tea. It was a nice tea — and the Christmas cake was good and tasted of spirits (Mum said she liked dogs with spirit) but I wasn't allowed any turkey. When Auntie Julia discovered the whopsie she wasn't very pleased, but she put a good face on it.

Chapter Four

I soon settled down in my new home (my tummy settled down too) but in January strange things began to happen: tea-chests and cardboard

boxes were all over the house and Mum spent a lot of time packing our belongings into them. We were going to move into town, she said. I wasn't very pleased — I'd done enough moving in my short life already — but I wasn't consulted. I was even less pleased when we moved into the flat — it was upstairs! The stairs in the house had been bad enough but these were dreadful. I firmly refused to go up them.

I had an awful day: I was stuck at the bottom of the stairs by the front door and nearly had the piano fall on me; you should have seen those men trying to heave it up that staircase! There was so much coming and going I was quite dizzy. Mum took no notice of me except to scold me for barking at all the men and I was beginning to wish I had stayed at the kennels; however, at last everyone left and Mum and I were alone again —only she was upstairs and I was downstairs! Not a very satisfactory arrangement, but I was determined I wasn't going to tackle that staircase.

That was when it began. The Battle-of-Wills. Mum won in the end of course — but only by carrying me up the stairs. She couldn't make me walk up them. That gave me an idea for a new strategy; if I refused to use my legs, I would have to be carried everywhere! I liked being carried; I liked to snuggle against Mum and put my chin on her shoulder and she would hold me tight. I felt safe. The strategy didn't work for long though.

The next day I was carried downstairs and taken for a walk (because we didn't have a garden, which I thought was pretty stupid) and when we came back I was left at the bottom of the stairs! Mum said I would have to stay there until I decided to come up on my own. She meant it too. She had that school-mistress tone of voice! (Did I tell you she was a teacher? Trust my luck! I liked her, but I would have had an easier life if my mistress hadn't been used to showing **authority**.)

I decided to test her of course, but by teatime there were delicious smells wafting down from the kitchen, and after I had squeaked pathetically to no avail I had to give in. It took some time to work out how I should tackle those stairs (they were much steeper and narrower than the ones at the house and it is very difficult when one is a long dog and a low-slung one into the bargain) but I got my brain working and found a way. It took a lot of doing but I managed it in the end. I have

'That was when it began.
The-Battle-of-Wills.'

6

my pride, but it wouldn't have done me much good if I had starved to death.

Having swallowed my pride and a very good tea (that's a figure-of-speech called 'syllepsis' — I know that because having a teacher for a mistress turned me into an educated dog as well as being aristocratic) I then went to my basket in the corridor and stayed there all evening. I certainly wasn't going to lower my dignity any further by keeping Mum company in the sitting-room and letting her think I didn't mind having lost a battle. (I made sure she carried my basket into her bedroom at night though!)

Chapter Five

Moving into town was quite nice but I quickly protested at being taken shopping; wherever I walked there were feet and legs and people tripping over me, and I didn't like being tied to a drainpipe when Mum went into the Co-op. Some dogs were stupid; they barked or cried when they were tied outside. I certainly wasn't going to let anyone see that I minded but I was anxious all the same, wondering whether I was going to be left there all day. (I hadn't forgotten the Battle of the Stairs when I had to stay by myself for so long!)

The best part of moving into town was the social life. I made quite a lot of friends down on the Batts by the river, where we went at least twice a day for our walks. At first I was very nervous about meeting new dogs; on the second day, when a giant Labrador came up to us, I slipped my collar and ran away as fast as my short legs would carry me (which wasn't very fast, as I'm not an athletic dog). However, I decided after a few days that this wouldn't do, for to run away like that is really beneath a Dachshund's dignity, so I adopted a new strategy: I would be friendly and invite the other dogs (even the giant ones) to play with me. It worked! All I had to do was to wag my tail furiously, move forward — and the other dogs would be completely disarmed; their hackles would come down and they would come to meet me and then we would have a good sniff at one another before having a game of 'chase me'.

I liked the Batts; there were lots of interesting smells because all kinds of dogs were taken there for their daily exercise. There was even a special dogs' toilet! In the summer I used to lie in the rock pools below the Falls and cool down. The reason I had to cool down was: I have a long coat as well as a long nose and a long back and a long tail, and I used to get very hot after running around with my friends.

When I first came to live with Mum she used to take me with her to school because she thought I would be lonely if I stayed by myself all day long. She used to leave me in the car and Auntie Sue would come and collect me and take me to her house until it was time to put me in the car again to go home. Mum thought that was a very good arrangement and I did too.

Auntie Sue lived in the school grounds; she had a garden, lots of Dachsies and a Dalmatian, so it was like being back at the kennels — even better, in fact, because we weren't made to stay outside all the time. She understood dogs and there was always lots to eat and plenty of titbits. She liked me especially because of my character; she thought I had personality and found me very amusing; I don't know why.

I liked playing with the Dalmatian; she was much bigger than I was but I like dogs who are bigger than I am because they are usually rough-but-gentle; that means they like chasing about and playing games but they don't bite! Everything changed though when Mum retired. I had to get used to a new routine and Mum had to get used to taking me out several times a day, and that's when I got to know the Batts so well and made so many new friends.

'There was even a dog's toilet.'
(x marks the spot).

8

Chapter Six

If you are a dog with personality you make enemies as well as friends. There were four dogs in our town who didn't seem to like me at all; they were very aggressive (rude with it too) and so I let them know that if that was the way they wanted things it was all right by me! I showed them in no uncertain terms just what I thought of them. There was never a fight though; I think fighting is stupid. Why risk getting battle-scarred if it's not necessary? If ever I did meet a dog who was off the lead, looking for a fight, I would inch my way backwards very slowly; in that way I could keep my dignity, running to safety only when he wasn't looking, when he'd decided I wasn't worth bothering with.

I had to be extra specially careful with Winston. He was called after a very-famous-man and I wasn't surprised; he certainly liked to show the other dogs in town that he was top-dog. Not that he went around showing off his superior position; he took it for granted that others would heed it and show respect and that didn't surprise me either: he was enormous! Mum said he was an Alsatian but he didn't look like one to me — he was much too big and black!

Winston's mistress was quite small, not much higher than he was, but she had a good-grip-on-him. Thank goodness! If we met in the Park I knew better than to bark at him to show I wasn't afraid (which was what I did with my enemies) because if he had decided to come for me his mistress wouldn't have kept her good-grip-on-him for long. So — my strategy was: I would briefly touch noses with him as politely as possible and then walk on (as close to Mum as I could). This worked at first, but Winston, being very intelligent, saw through this plan and decided to prolong the agony. Not that he was an unkind dog; he just liked to tease me and make quite sure that I knew my place.

The way Winston prolonged the agony was: instead of letting me walk past him he used to give me a few nudges in the ribs! When he had reduced me to a quivering jelly his mistress used to say, 'Now, Winston, don't tease poor Basil,' and Mum used to say, 'He won't really hurt you, Bas,' but she didn't sound very convinced). When he had teased me enough for one day and moved on, I had enough sense not to slip my collar and run, because he would have known and would have come after me as sure as my name isn't Boris! Mum said I was very sensible just to walk on very slowly and that it was by far the best thing to do. It certainly worked, because it showed Winston that I had a healthy respect for him, and that was all he wanted to know.

Tarka was even bigger than Winston but she was a good friend. She was a very great Dane, almost as high as Mum, and we used to have a good romp together. Sometimes, when I was visiting Auntie Christine, she would take my lead in her mouth and pretend she was my mistress, taking me for a walk all round the house!

Tarka was only a puppy, but I fell in love at a very early age with Becky, an Old English Sheepdog who lived down the road. It never came to anything though. Just when she was beginning to respond to my advances she would disappear for three weeks. I used to sit by her gate, waiting for her, and Mum used to feel very sorry for me, but in the end I got tired of playing the waiting game; it's only stupid dogs who don't get the message that they're not welcome.

Chapter Seven

When Mum first retired she and Auntie Isabel used to take me for long walks and we would end up getting lost and come home **exhausted**. Once we got on to a very busy road and I was so scared by the big lorries that I refused to walk and Mum had to keep picking me up and carrying me. She wasn't very pleased about it, because even when I was a young dog and without a middle-age-spread I was very heavy.

When Auntie Isabel moved house and went to live miles away, the long walks stopped (except when Auntie Robin came to stay) and Mum used to take me to the Bowling Green instead. I found that pretty boring and so when I thought we'd been there long enough I would run on to the Green and tell her that it was time to go home. I wasn't very popular when I did that, because dogs aren't allowed on the Green, and I soon found out that it was dangerous too. It's not very pleasant being bowled at by a big, round, hard ball that can't keep a straight line and so you can't get out of the way! In the end I was banished to the park and had to watch through the railings (when I wasn't playing with other dogs) but it didn't work very well because people kept leaving the gate open and I would seize my opportunity to come in again pretty quick smart.

I always knew when it was Sunday. Mum would put the alarm on, get dressed quickly and take me for a quick walk, then she would say, 'I'm going to church now, Basil; I'll be back soon.'

When she came back it was time to go to Auntie Freda's for a coffee. Auntie Freda lived opposite us and she understood dogs so I used to look forward to Sundays because there were always plenty of titbits. She used to make buttered-toast-and-marmalade specially for me to eat whilst she and Mum talked non-stop. When she moved away because she was old and couldn't manage her stairs any longer (which didn't surprise me one bit) I missed her very much — and Mum did too.

People were always moving away; Auntie Lorraine had been the first to go (she was the one who christened me 'Basil of the Batts') and then Auntie Julia left. Just when I got used to them and decided to be friendly instead of ignoring them they would disappear! If I disappeared Mum would get cross because she had to go and look for me — but I soon learnt that there's one law for humans and another one for dogs.

Chapter Eight

Soon after we came to live in town Mum went away for a holiday and I went to stay with Auntie Monica. It was **all right**! There was another dog to play with and food in the bowls all day long, and I was allowed to go out whenever I pleased on to the village green. One day I decided to explore; it wasn't a good idea, though, because I met a farm-dog and

tried to make friends with him but he wasn't having any; before you could say 'Basil Hume' he rushed at me and attacked me.

I hadn't been assaulted before and it wasn't a nice experience, I can tell you. I went back to Auntie Monica's but I didn't tell her what had happened — I was too proud to do that. Two days later, she caught me licking my wounds (I'd had more than my feelings hurt) and took me to the doctor's. He said I had to wear a bucket so that I couldn't lick the wound any more and make it worse.

Have you ever had to wear a bucket on your head? It's not very nice, I can tell you. When Mum came back, Auntie Monica had to break the news to her very gently so that she wouldn't be too shocked on being greeted by a yellow bucket instead of a long black Roman nose. She felt very sorry for me, more because she knew how much I hated losing my dignity than because of my septic bottom. However, I showed her that I would carry the situation off with my usual aplomb; I held my head high and walked with a swagger.

It isn't very easy to eat when you're wearing a bucket but I

'Very embarrassing, really.'

12

'She even took to smoking cigars!'

managed it; the main bother was that it stopped me from having my usual sniffing sessions when we went for walks. (Mum said she was pleased about that, anyway.) At first I didn't much care to be seen on the Batts with a bucket for a head and I was afraid my friends would laugh at me or even not recognise me, but it wasn't the dogs who turned out to be the problem, it was the humans. You wouldn't credit how stupid some humans can be. One day I was walking down the Wynd, where we lived, a few yards behind Mum as usual, and had stopped to try to have a sniff when a woman saw me:

'He's got a bucket on his head!' she said.

'I know,' said Mum.

'You know?'

Mum and I looked at each other. Really, how stupid can one get?

Most people were kind; some would stop and say, 'Poor thing!' Others would pretend not to notice, not wanting to embarrass me. A few would laugh but I didn't mind; they didn't mean any harm and I suppose I did look comical. The rude people who just stared I treated with true Basil Fawlty disdain.

We got to know quite a lot of people during those three weeks. I became quite famous and our regular acquaintances would stop and enquire anxiously how I was progressing. That was the beginning of how I came to be so **well-known** — that and the fact that Mum was beginning to make quite a name for herself; she even took to smoking cigars! Very embarrassing really.

When the bucket came off there was general rejoicing, not least by yours truly Basil. I was given the all-clear. Thank goodness, I thought; no more visits to the doctor's.

Chapter Nine

I can't imagine any self-respecting dog enjoying going to the doctor's; I certainly didn't. You should have seen the fuss some dogs made. They would have to be dragged up the stairs and then they would sit shivering with fear next to their owners until it was their turn to be called.

I used to like the first part, being in the waiting-room, for there were lots of interesting smells and other dogs to go up to and make friends with (except that they were too miserable to want to play). It was another matter though when it was my turn to go into the surgery. I firmly refused to move an inch! It wasn't that I was afraid of course; I would hide under the chair only so that Mum would have to coax me out, and the only reason I refused to use my legs was so that she would have to carry me. I was on to a good thing there because there wasn't time to have a Battle-of-Wills so I always won.

'Really, Basil!' the Vet-Doctor would say, whilst Mum tried to hide her embarrassment at being seen to let a dog get the better of her. Once I'd been lifted on to the table I was always perfectly well-behaved so that Mum ended by being proud of me; she would hold me and kiss me and soothe me whilst the doctor prodded and squeezed and stuck needles into me.

It was all a great fuss about nothing, I thought, as I walked out of the door. That was, until I had to wear the bucket again! However, I'd lived through it once so I supposed I could do it again, and it did get me a lot of sympathy.

The reason why I had to wear the bucket again was: I had Anal-Gland-Trouble. Not very nice, and certainly not something that could be mentioned in the drawing-room. However, it was a fact of life and Dachshunds are very prone to that particular fact (because we're so long). I had to wear a bucket because I spent all the time licking where it was sore — when Mum wasn't looking.

I had Anal-Gland-Trouble several times a year, which meant that a good third of my life was spent with a bucket on my head. 'Not again!' people would say. 'Poor Basil!' Mum became quite grumpy about having to take a plastic-headed dog for walks, particularly when they changed the bucket to a lamp-shade which scraped along the ground; that was because I'm low as well as being long. In the end she agreed to an operation. I didn't like the sound of it at all, but I wasn't consulted.

Have you ever had your Anal-Glands removed? Don't! That's all I'm going to say about it. I have to admit that it was worth it in the end but I prefer not to talk about the immediate post-operative effects. I know most people (dogs too) like to talk about their operation, sparing no details, but this is the exception to the rule. All I will say is: Mum felt very sorry for me indeed.

Chapter Ten

Mum had quickly learnt to understand what I was saying, on the occasions when I needed to make my wishes and feelings known. I

very rarely had to raise my voice to her and she was very good at understanding body-language, at which I was a past master. Usually it was sufficient for me to come into the room and sit and look fixedly at her until she took notice of me, but sometimes I had to utter a few squeaks before she would look up and ask me what I wanted. Very occasionally I had to give a bark.

I could put a lot of expression into my barks. If there was an intruder I could make a lot of noise. Because I have a very deep bark, and people who don't know me think on hearing me that I must be very big and fierce, this had the effect of frightening some people, but soon the ones who were going down the Wynd became used to seeing me sitting there by our entrance, warning them off; they either took no notice or just said, 'Hello, Basil!' Mum's friends weren't afraid of me either, even though I barked at them from the top of the stairs when they came in. I suppose the fact that I usually wagged my tail at the same time had something to do with it.

One bark was usually all that was needed to make Mum do what I wanted. I could put quite a note of indignation into it sometimes, particularly when I went with her to play bridge at Auntie Joan's. I didn't play bridge of course, because I'm not really a games-playing dog, but I always went along. Usually I lay under the table but people's feet were a nuisance; every so often I received a kick followed by 'Sorry, Basil, I forgot you were there!' (Uncle Nigel was very bad at this because he was long, like me.) Eventually I'd look for a safer spot to lie in until supper-time.

Supper-time at Auntie Joan's meant **good food**. She always had a plate of tasty titbits for me. Sometimes though I had to remind her of the time (humans don't seem to have a clock in their stomachs like dogs) so I would startle them all by giving a sudden, loud bark.

'Gracious! It's supper-time!' Auntie Joan would exclaim, hurrying into the kitchen (which I had previously explored just to make sure she hadn't forgotten my plate). The cards would be cleared away and food laid on the table and then they would start talking ten to the dozen and forget all about me again! I used to give them plenty of chance, sitting quietly and expectantly by Auntie Joan's chair next to the trolley, but eventually I would become quite indignant at being forgotten. A series of single barks usually did the trick.

'My goodness!' Auntie Joan would exclaim. 'I've forgotten Basil!' She would then sit and feed me whilst Mum wolfed her sandwiches and said, 'Really, Basil, you are a naughty dog!' I knew better than to ask Mum for titbits, though she was very good at giving me scraps of fat off her meat and would usually give me the last morsel of biscuit she was eating. I'm a very good-mannered dog really and usually wait until I'm asked, but Auntie Joan was a soft-touch and naturally I took advantage, especially as I knew she wouldn't scold me.

Chapter Eleven

I had soon learnt to understand a few words of English, such as 'no!' and 'come here'. 'Come here' meant 'stay where you are so that I can come and fetch you even though you are a hundred yards away!' I knew that when Mum said 'No!' she meant it, so I didn't see much point in arguing with her on that score. I knew what 'stay' meant too (it meant the same as 'come here'), but the best word she used was 'car'.

I love cars. They are good places to go to sleep in, nice and warm and soothing, and in Mum's car I had my own special place in the back where I could stretch out on my blanket. Everyone said what a good dog I was in the car. That was because I kept so quiet no-one knew I was there until we stopped and Mum spoke to me.

Once, when we first came to town, I had an adventure. I decided to see what was at the top of the Wynd where we lived so I set out late one afternoon to explore. I soon discovered it had not been a good idea, because at the top was a big road with lots of people and traffic; I decided to look for a safe place to hide in and then I found the **ideal thing**: I came upon a Garage with lots of cars so I slipped into one of them when the man wasn't looking and lay on the floor by the front seat. When the owner came to drive the car away he was very surprised to find an aristocratic black dog lying there. As it happened, my name and telephone number were on my collar so Mum received a phone call, 'Skipper's garage here; we have a dog called Basil in one of our cars and he won't come out!' (Mum told me that later when she came to collect me.) Everyone seemed to think it was very funny, I don't know why.

One reason I liked going in the car with Mum was that she had to lift me. The first time she said 'Jump in' I looked at her in surprise. 'Do you really expect me to jump as high as that?' I asked, looking at the shelf under the open hatch-back. It wasn't in fact any higher than her bed and I could jump on to that all right, but she was in a hurry and had no time to argue.

'Very well,' she said, 'I'll lift you up just for this once.' It hadn't taken me very long to win that particular battle! I had her just where I wanted on that particular matter, and ever after that she carried me into the car and I could snuggle against her. I didn't mind being put into the back and then ignored, because we had had **close contact** before that so I felt loved and contented as well as being self-satisfied and pleased at having got my own way.

Mum and I had a good relationship and I loved her really, especially when we had a good cuddle (which we always did before she put me to bed) but sometimes life at home got a **bit too much**. It got a bit too much particularly when we had a Battle-of-Wills about going for walks. The trouble was: I didn't always want to go when she wanted me to and she didn't always want to go when I wanted her to. This made her **irritable**. So when it was time to go to stay with Auntie Joan because Mum was going away and dogs-weren't-welcome, it was a bit of a relief.

Auntie Joan always made a big fuss of me. Not that she was sloppy and expected me to be affectionate; she just loved dogs and me in particular and she understood my aristocratic nature — so I liked going to stay with her. What is more, I didn't have to go up any stairs and she had a garden. I loved Mum best of course but it's a good thing occasionally to have a break! Mum thought so too.

Poor old Mum! I did lead her a dance and try her patience. Most of the time the trouble was that she was always in a hurry whilst I believed in taking my time and going through life at my own pace. Because she was always in a hurry and had lots of things to do, we didn't have long conversations together; I'm not a very talkative dog anyway (certainly not chatty, like some of those yappy little dogs I've met on the Batts). She and I understood each other though.

Chapter Twelve

When we moved into town and Mum started having a Social Life I was not pleased at being left alone when she went out in the evenings. I waited until she moved out of earshot and then I howled for a while. This didn't seem to do any good so I scratched at the carpet (it made a hole which had to be covered with a mat). The neighbours split on me of course, telling Mum how badly behaved I was when she was out, so she wasn't very pleased with me. She refused to stop going out and leaving me so she compromised; she let me lie on her bed when she wasn't there. It always pays to persevere; you get there in the end!

Sometimes this question of leaving me alone got too much of a good thing. Mum had joined the Dramatic Society and if she was in a play and had to rehearse every evening I would begin to get very indignant indeed. Sometimes I decided I would just show her, so instead of being there to greet her at the top of the stairs when she came back I used to stay on the bed looking reproachful. Towards the end though, when she'd been out several evenings in a row, my temper would begin to boil (it takes a lot to make me angry, I can tell you) and I would go into the kitchen and upset my food and water bowls. At first Mum thought this was an accident, but when it happened often she began to realise I had had a tantrum!

She had tried taking me with her to rehearsals but I embarrassed her too much. At first I used to sit quietly and watch, but when people started running about on the 'stage' I didn't like it at all and I used to dart into the middle of them and bark **menacingly**. Everyone would laugh, but Mum said I was being a nuisance and tied me to the leg of a chair and said she wouldn't take me again . . . I don't know why she thought she was any good at acting: she could never fool me.

One thing I learnt about her, though, was that she could be trusted. If she said she would come back she meant it. So I wasn't too worried one night when she shut me in the garage. I didn't know why she wanted me to stay there in the dark but I knew she would come back in the end and let me out so I just sat there quietly, although I wasn't very pleased, I can tell you. Well, she left me there a very long time and it was a long way past my bedtime.

At last I heard her calling 'Basil!' She sounded quite worried and I thought, 'I'll bet she's forgotten she's shut me in the garage,' so I gave a little 'woof' — just to tell her where I was. She was very pleased to see me, and I was certainly glad to see her. There she was in her dressing-gown and slippers, shivering in the cold, saying, 'Poor Basil! I didn't realise I'd shut the garage door on you. Why didn't you let me know you were there?'

She told me she'd been walking up and down the Wynd at regular intervals since midnight, looking for me; she had thought I might have gone to my girl-friend's. Really! You would think she would have looked in the most obvious place, wouldn't you?

'This question of leaving me alone got too much of a good thing.'

19

Chapter Thirteen

Apart from 'you know what' and various other bucket episodes because of eczema, I have been quite a healthy dog except that after my operation I developed a Heart-Murmur. It didn't worry me, in fact it was quite a **good thing** because it frightened Mum into carrying me up the stairs for a while, until she got tired of it and decided I wasn't going to have a heart attack. The time came, though, when I developed Old-Man-Trouble. The doctor said that was probably what the matter was and that he needed a specimen. I don't know what he needed a specimen of, and I didn't take much notice, but suddenly Mum began to behave very **oddly**.

I really found it most embarrassing, she behaved so peculiarly. When I went down the Wynd for my late-night wee and was hoping for a chance encounter with my girl-friend, the Old English Sheepdog, she insisted on coming with me. That in itself was odd, because she would usually just stand by the entrance to the Mews and watch until I had done my wee, and then she would firmly put me on the lead and force me to go back in, saying she was cold. Well this time she announced we were going for a walk; naturally I made no objection, but every time I stopped to lift my leg she dived underneath me with a small shovel on the end of a plastic bottle! When I looked at her in amazement all she said was 'Blast!' By the time we had gone round the block, with several repeat performances, she was becoming quite bad-tempered and frankly I was beginning to worry about her.

The next morning she made me go round the Castle Walk, (hoping, she said afterwards, there wouldn't be many people there at that time of day). I wasn't pleased at this disruption to my routine, for we normally walked down the steps and along Park Wynd and I liked to meet the regulars. I was even less pleased when we had a repeat performance of the night before. Every time I stopped she bent down with her shovel and tried to push it under me if I attempted to cock my leg! A couple came past at one point and she pretended she was doing up her shoe-lace. All this was beginning to make me very edgy and my bladder was getting very full because it's off-putting to have something pushed under you when you're about to do a wee. In the end I had to stop and do a very long one, despite the presence of the ubiquitous shovel. Mum got it all over her hand (serve her right, I thought) but she seemed satisfied at last because some of it had gone into the bottle, and I was unceremoniously turned around to head for home, calling at a friend's house on the way back so that Mum could wash her hands.

Once we had arrived home I became even more worried because Mum then subsided into giggles. I ask you! I didn't see anything funny about it at all: I found the whole episode distasteful. I was very fond of her but she did have an odd sense-of-humour.

The result of all that palaver was another visit to the doctor's. He said I was to have hormones, female ones, and told Mum not to be surprised if I began to squat instead of lifting my leg. That wiped the smile off her face! She said she was afraid I wouldn't know if I was Arthur or Martha. Goodness knows what she was talking about; I know I'm not a very brainy Dachshund (even if I am an educated one) but I do know my own name.

Chapter Fourteen

No-one ever credits me with much intelligence. 'Basil isn't as bright as Tickey was,' Mum would say to her friends, 'but he's a plodder.'

Fancy being compared all the time to one's predecessor! From what I could gather, Tickey — who was supposed to be so marvellous — was very stupid. For one thing he used to chase cars. Not only do I like cars (when I'm being taken for a ride) — I have a very healthy respect for them because I know they are **dangerous**. I know this because

when we first came to live in town one came along the Wynd and bumped me. I had decided to venture out of our courtyard and do a bit of exploring to see if there were any interesting smells when suddenly I was bumped. I didn't tell Mum of course, for she would have said, 'Serve you right,' but Auntie Dora saw it happen and told her about it. Anyway, it taught me a lesson. After that, when we were out walking, if I saw a car coming I would stop and tell Mum to put me on the lead so that I could feel safe.

However, to get back to Tickey. Another reason I think he was stupid was: he used to get into fights. I ask you, fancy a dog the size of a threepenny bit taking on the big dogs who came to attack him! Myself, I think discretion is the better part of valour, and I'm much bigger than he was — I'm a well-built **standard** Dachshund. I call it being well-built but some people were very rude and said I was getting fat. I may have put on a few inches after my operation but I certainly wasn't flabby — very solid in fact (which was why Mum didn't like carrying me).

Mum did admit that even Tickey wasn't as intelligent as his older step-brother Murphy had been. Now I ask you, fancy calling a German Shepherd Dog after an Irish potato! Mum said she hadn't christened him — but she made the same excuse about my name.

Even if I'm not brainy I reckon I'm very intelligent; one has to be to think out the sort of strategies I thought out. Talking of intelligence, I was really disgusted one day when we were going along the Castle

Walk. For once Mum wasn't in a hurry; she was enjoying the warm sunshine and I was enjoying my sniffs along the edge which looked down on to the river, and we were both in a good mood. Then a man and a woman came along and the woman was saying, 'You'd think they would put a railing up, wouldn't you? It's very dangerous; anyone could fall over the edge.'

Well! I looked at Mum and Mum looked at me.

'Did you hear that?' I said.

'They were southerners,' Mum said; 'that accounts for it.' She was very incensed.

She told a man who was sitting on a bench nearby how incensed she was but she chose the wrong man to say it to, because he was a southerner too! However, having put one foot in it she decided to put the other foot in as well and said, 'They must think that northerners are very unintelligent. As if we would let our children or our dogs go near the edge unless we could trust them!'

I agreed with her; she always trusted me to be sensible, and railings would have spoilt the aesthetic beauty (Mum taught me that word 'aesthetic') of the Castle Walk.

The incident put her in a bad mood and she muttered about it all the way home. I must say I sympathised with her on that occasion.

Mum was very good about trusting me to be sensible; she wasn't always screeching, 'Basil, don't go there! Look what you're doing! Be careful!' She knew better than to turn me into a neurotic dog.

Another good thing about her was: if we went near the river she let me go in the water (except that she was always nagging at me to swim). Now why should she want me to swim? I couldn't see any point in it — I tried it once and it used up too much energy. I liked to paddle in, a few feet from the edge, and lie down and have a little drink. I could never understand though why I was scolded when I walked through puddles. They are water!

'Oh, good! A puddle!'

23

Chapter Fifteen

Do you like snow? I do. One year it was very deep and I had a lot of fun one morning playing hide-and-seek in it with a brown Labrador we met on the Batts. I don't know what got into Mum though. One minute she was talking with the Labrador's mistress and her children and the next minute she was sitting on a plastic tray and before you could say 'Basil Fawlty' she had disappeared! When I looked again she was at the bottom of the slope, lying in the snow and giggling.

'Second childhood!' said the Labrador, knowingly. Well! That obviously accounted for her oddness. After that incident I pretended not to know her and we went on with our game of hide-and-seek; I even refused to come home when Mum wanted me to, so the Labrador's mistress offered to bring me back later and I stayed for another half-hour.

Did I regret it! When I turned up at our front door I was exhausted.

'Basil!' Mum exclaimed. 'Look at you! How am I going to get all those snowballs off you?'

I felt very sorry for myself, I can tell you. I was getting frost-bite in some very delicate places.

'It's no good trying to pull the snowballs off me,' I said to her. 'You'll have to think of some other way.'

Then Mum had a bright idea. She carried me up the stairs and put me in a warm bath. Oh, the bliss of it! When all the snowballs had melted I was wrapped in a warm towel and put in my basket. I decided to give the snow a miss after that. Fortunately by the next day it had begun to go away, otherwise when Mum wanted me to go out there would have been another Battle-of-Wills.

Another thing I like is being groomed. This didn't happen as often as it should because Mum was usually too busy or too tired, but when she did bring out the brush and comb I knew I was in for a blissful ten minutes.

I would lie on my side and Mum would kneel down and set to work. 'Goodness, Basil!' she'd say. 'Look at all this hair that's coming off you. I really ought to comb you more regularly.' If I'd been a show-dog of course she would have done, but although I had a good pedigree I wasn't good enough to be shown, because I'm too black; I have a little red on my jowls and under my tail where it meets my body — which is an unfortunate place to have it, rather embarrassing really — but that apparently isn't enough.

When Mum had finished combing one side of me she would haul me over on to my other side and go through the same procedure (by this time I was always too **somnolent** to turn over on my own). Soon there would be enough black fluff on the newspaper beside us to fill a cushion almost, and I would be told how beautiful I looked; I was certainly much slimmer after it! However, my coat never remained sleek for long, but it's personality that counts, isn't it?

Thank goodness Mum never took me to the Poodle Parlour. Her friend, Auntie Gloria in Africa, once took her Pekinese to be clipped (because her big dog had chewed it) and he came home totally bald!

Chapter Sixteen

Did you know that dogs have Psychiatrists as well as Vet-Doctors? Don't make any mistake — I didn't have an attack of insanity but Mum did have to call in the doggie-psychiatrist shortly after my operation. I suppose I had a kind of Nervous Breakdown.

One day, when my heart was murmuring pretty loudly, Mum was on the telephone and I was struggling to get up the stairs. Well, I stuck halfway up! It was a frightening experience, I can tell you. I squeaked and squeaked but you know what women are like when they get on the phone; it was ages and ages (at least thirty seconds) before Mum realised something was up. She came to my rescue of course but **that was it**, I decided; in no way was I going to climb those stairs again.

The next time I was at the bottom of that staircase I absolutely refused to come up. For a few days after that I was carried up but Mum wasn't very pleased about it and I didn't feel very safe because she was getting older and I was getting fatter and heavier, and she was staggering all over the place with me.

'Basil,' she said, 'I think you are playing me up. You are just going to have to change your attitude because I'm not carrying you up the stairs any longer.'

She meant business (she was using her school-mistress tone) but two can play at that game. I decided it was time for another Battle-of-Wills. Besides that, she didn't seem to understand that I was suffering from Panic-Attacks. It's not very pleasant to find oneself stuck halfway up a staircase. So I stayed at the bottom, and this time not even the thought of food would tempt me up. She tried, in the end, putting my feeding bowl at the top of the stairs as a ploy (Mum's word for 'strategy') but it was of no use: I stayed where I was.

I stayed there for the rest of that night and the next day! Mum relented enough to put my food downstairs the next evening, but after that she said I would have to make an effort to come upstairs for it, otherwise we were going to spend the rest of our lives apart, with me at the bottom and her at the top. However, in no way was I going to make that effort! Before she went to bed she tried dangling a tasty morsel of ham on the end of a piece of string, hoping that would lure me up. Then she placed it on a low step, hoping that I would at least attempt the bottom few rungs of the metaphorical ladder!

I was getting pretty fed-up myself by now so I did make a half-hearted try, but it was no good; my nerve had gone. In the end Mum had to give in (being soft-hearted despite seeming stern) and start carrying me up again.

One day, however, a strange man came to the door. She had called at the A1 Kennels (without consulting me) to ask Mister Simpson, the doggie-psychiatrist, if he could help. In he walked and asked her what the trouble was exactly. She explained and said, 'I don't know if he's playing me up or not,' (as if I would!)

'Have you got his lead?' asked the psychiatrist, and he put it on me and walked up the stairs with me following behind him attached to the lead. You should have seen Mum's face!

'I would never have thought of that,' she said. (I can't think why not; I thought it should have been obvious, because she knew I liked to have my lead on when I wasn't feeling safe.)

Mister Simpson made me walk up the stairs on the lead once or twice, and each time we reached the top I got all the 'what a good dog' baloney, but I wagged my tail and looked pleased and Mum was happier — for the time being. She told all her friends about it and I told my friends, and suggested that some of them who had problems

'Now what exactly is the problem?'

should visit Mister Simpson. It became quite a conversation piece. However, it all became rather a nuisance as Mum's patience began to wear thin. She would give a sigh every time she was summoned by my squeak to come downstairs and put me on the lead, and I used to be so slow she would become quite frustrated. 'Hurry up, Basil!' she would say, because her coffee was getting cold or she was in the middle of a conversation with a friend.

Then one day the balloon went up! She caught me coming up the stairs on my own, trying to sneak past her into the kitchen.

'You **have** been playing me up!' she said. 'That's it! You're not getting away with it any longer.' (I was given no credit for initiative.)

I did though! She had to relent when she stood at the top of the stairs and watched me pathetically try to struggle up, stopping every few steps for a breather. In the end she would go for the lead and help me along.

Chapter Seventeen.

As well as having a Vet-Doctor and a Psychiatrist, I also had a Dentist. One day I got a huge piece of bone stuck between my teeth and no matter how much Mum tried she couldn't pull it out.

'It's no good, Basil,' she said; 'you'll just have to be patient until I can call in the dentist.'

I wasn't very pleased about that; I had heard my friends say that their mistresses didn't like going to the dentist and that it turned them into quivering jellies; however, when he came, and it turned out to be Uncle Mick, I didn't mind, because he was firm-but-gentle. He borrowed our pliers and yanked out the piece of bone in one shake of a dog's tail, as the saying goes. Mum said that it takes an expert to do that.

I used to like it when Auntie Robin came to stay, except when

'I stopped and gave her my fixed look'

28

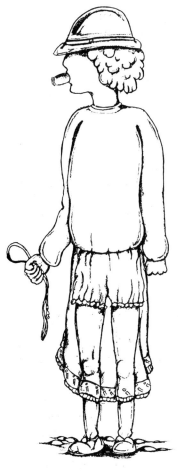

she locked us all out of the flat late one night and Mum had to go to a public phone-box and dial nine-nine-nine for the Police (who seemed to think it was very amusing). Auntie Robin was a Psychologist and so she understood dogs and always made a great fuss of me (without being too sloppy). She seemed to understand Mum too, which was more than I did sometimes.

As she grew older Mum really began to worry me, she was becoming so odd. One day in the summer she embarrassed me so much I spoke to my friends about it; they said it was because she was growing **absent-minded** and perhaps she ought to call in Mister Simpson so that he could put her mind back again where it ought to be.

What happened on this particular day was: I needed to go out and so I was trying to hurry her up whilst she got dressed. She had something on her mind which certainly wasn't me but she eventually realised that I was getting **desperate**, so she hurried up and took me out. When we were halfway down the Wynd I suddenly realised she wasn't dressed! It was very embarrassing. I stopped and gave her my fixed look.

'Oh, my goodness!' she exclaimed. 'I've forgotten to put my skirt on! No wonder my legs felt cold.'

We hurried back home immediately and I was very glad none of my friends had seen her.

The trouble was, things got worse. She became very absent-minded and started forgetting me all over the place. She would take me with her to meetings and then leave without me.

'Aren't you taking Basil home with you?' someone would say, and she would exclaim,

29

'Oh, my goodness! Poor Bas! I'd forgotten you were there.' (This was because I was so well-behaved and quiet.)

It was just the same when we went for our walks. Mum would stride along deep in thought and suddenly realise I wasn't with her. This always made her cross because she wanted to get back home and get on with all the things she had to do, whereas I don't like to be hurried; that isn't what a dog's life is about. Usually I ignored her, knowing she would have to come back and fetch me, but one day I fooled her. She stood near the top of the steps leading to the Batts and called me several times. When there was no response she looked into the distance and yelled, 'Basil, come on!!' Well, at last I had witnesses as to the state of her mental health because a couple who were passing stopped and looked at her in amazement.

'He's by your feet,' the woman said. Mum did feel a fool.

'Why didn't you tell me you were there?' she said to me indignantly. (Not a word of praise to me for being a good dog!)

Chapter Eighteen

We used to go for doggie-walks quite often with Auntie Lynne and Sally. Sally and I liked each other's company but didn't have much in common to talk about (she's a Spaniel and very fast on her feet, whereas I'm a slow dog) so after saying 'Hello' to each other we left it at that and went our own ways. She would run on ahead and I would dawdle, taking my time and having a good sniff.

Mum and Auntie Lynne would talk to each other non-stop whilst they were walking; usually they suddenly remembered that I was supposed to be with them and would stop and wait for me to catch up, but one day they were so deep in conversation they forgot all about me. When I looked up from a particularly intriguing smell they were **miles** away. I knew I would never catch up with them so I decided to go home.

I was a bit hurt that Mum had forgotten me, so when she appeared at last and found me sitting by our front door I gave her one of my looks. When she said, 'There you are, you naughty dog,' I put my head in the air and pretended I was in a huff. Actually, I was rather proud of myself for having found my way home, but although Mum too was quite proud of my initiative it was beneath her dignity to say so;

instead she said that the walk had in fact been far better without me, because she didn't have to keep stopping — which wasn't a very nice thing to say at all. If that's the way she feels, I thought, she can go by herself the next time! (I wasn't too bothered about going for walks anyway; give me a car-ride any time; it's much less exhausting.)

'I wasn't bothered about going for walks anyway.'

So, the next time she wanted me to go walking with Auntie Lynne I decided to stay at home. She lured me into it though under false pretences by putting me in the car. However, when the car stopped and Sally came to greet me I was glad I had come, because Sally was in an interesting condition and was very flirtatious. She had me chasing her all round the racecourse. (I'd often wondered why it was called a 'racecourse'; now I understood.) I lost a few pounds that day, I can tell you.

The same thing happened with Auntie Marjorie's dog, Sophie, another time. Sophie was a giant Retriever so her mum and mine thought it very funny that I should entertain any hopes. They were very embarrassed though when we were walking through town on our way back and I caught Sophie unawares! It didn't get me very far, but Mum and Auntie Marjorie walked quickly on ahead, pretending not to know me.

Chapter Nineteen

Did I tell you my mistress had bad habits? She used to complain about having to take me out three times a day, but every day she had three ports of call: the Off-Licence, the News-Agent's and the Betting-Shop. I ask you, fancy being owned by somebody as degenerate as that!

She didn't even buy 'The Times' when she went to the News-Agent's, she bought 'The Sporting Life'. Mind you, although I'm not a betting dog myself I didn't object to going to the Betting-Shop with

'I know, she'll have gone to the Bookie's next door.'

her. It was nice and warm in there and when it was time to leave she always had to drag me out. They all thought that was very amusing. What they didn't know was: when they had been thinking I was lying there in a comatose state I was in fact keeping my ears open for tips. One day I picked up a very good one; there was a horse running called Just Basil. I tried to tell Mum to put something on it but she wouldn't listen. Just as well, as it happened, because it came in last.

One good thing about Mum's bad habits was: I always knew where to look for her if I got lost. One day she was in the Book-Shop on Castle Hill and got so carried away browsing she forgot all about me, as usual, and walked out of the shop without me. 'I know,' I said to myself; 'she'll have gone to the Bookie's next door.' That was pretty smart thinking, only she wasn't there. People were pretty surprised to see an aristocratic Dachshund enter the Betting-Shop but one of the regulars who knew me said, 'Hello, Basil, where's your mistress?'

'You tell me,' I wanted to reply, but he didn't understand Dachsie language.

He told everyone that it was all right, he knew where I lived and would take me home, so I was marched through the Market Place on the end of a piece of string (I ask you!) and tied to the handle of our front door because Mum wasn't in.

Well, what an indignity! I was very glad when Mum turned up at

'People were pretty surprised to see an aristocratic Dachshund enter the Betting Shop.'

last and set me free. I gave her my 'where do you think you've been?' look, expecting her to apologise, but all she said was, 'There you are, Basil! Why are you tied to the door-handle with a piece of string?'

She had been looking for me all over town, she said, and had already been back to the flat twice to see if I had turned up.

Mum spent the rest of the day wondering who had tied me to the door-handle; I wasn't going to tell her; it was an episode I preferred to forget. She found out much later on one of her trips to the Bookie's:

'By the way,' Uncle Len said, 'I took Basil home for you a few weeks ago; he had lost you.'

She didn't of course tell him that it was she who had lost me, forgetting me like that. There's no justice in a dog's life. The trouble with being a good, quiet, well-behaved Dachshund, in keeping with my aristocratic nature, is that you get taken advantage of.

Mum did have some good habits though, as well as bad ones. When she first retired she used to spend a lot of time working for Oxfam (whatever that might be) and I used to go along to the shop with her and help. The way I helped was: I would sit in the shop whilst she was busy unpacking lots of cardboard boxes and putting things on shelves, and people passing by would be lured in through the door on seeing an aristocratic Dachshund sitting there, and they would come in and make a fuss of me — and then they would decide to buy something! I became quite an institution.

The Oxfam shop was at the bottom of the Wynd, so Mum could easily pop along whenever she received a phone call to say that more boxes had arrived. The trouble was, she had to spend more and more time there, almost as much as she spent at the Bookie's, and what with accompanying her to Oxfam one minute and being dragged to the Betting-shop the next I never knew whether I was coming or going.

Well, one afternoon we had gone for a quick walk, and I had stopped to have a chin-and-tail-wag with one of my acquaintances and when I looked up Mum was nowhere to be seen. I certainly wasn't going to the Bookie's to look for her (not after the episode with the piece of string — even though Mum did say it had been very kind of Uncle Len to go to so much trouble) so I went into the Oxfam Shop and sat and waited for her there, feeling sure she would turn up sooner or later.

At first no-one took much notice, except to say 'Hello, Basil', thinking that Mum must be somewhere around, but when it came to closing-time the other helpers decided they had better take me home. 'Come along, Basil,' they said. 'We have to lock up now.'

Well I certainly wasn't going to go just because they wanted me to, and in any case I wasn't going to risk being tied to the door-handle again. I dug my toes in and said politely,

'No, thank you; I'll wait here until Mum comes.'

In the end they had to leave me there and call at our flat on their way home to tell Mum where I was. She, of course, had been looking for me and had just gone back to the flat, wondering where to look next. As it happened, she had taken a day off from going to the Oxfam Shop, so it hadn't occurred to her that I might have been there.

Mum and the other helpers had a good laugh, but I didn't think it was funny: 'You might have told me you weren't coming here today!' I said to her indignantly, when she came to collect me, but I was very pleased to see her, all the same!

Chapter Twenty

Fortunately, as I said, I was very well-known, famous in fact. When people saw us together they would say, 'Hello, Basil,' and virtually ignore Mum's presence. Usually I would stalk past with my head in the air and be scolded for my bad manners, but noblesse sometimes has to oblige, and if I was in a good mood — that is, if I hadn't been dragged around town and trodden on (I can't help having large feet) — I would acknowledge the greeting by a faint movement of my tail.

There were a few people I really liked though, and when they greeted me I would forget my dignity and give them a really good tail-wag and lots of kisses. Mum said they were very honoured.

The reason why being so well-known was a good thing was: if Mum lost me (which was happening far too often for my liking) someone was sure to come along and rescue me eventually. One day Jean-the-Traffic-Warden saw me go into Blaney's, the Off-Licence, to see if Mum was there.

'Hello, Basil,' she said. 'Where's your mum?'

'That's just what I want to know,' I replied. (The traffic warden was a Dachsie person so she could understand me.)

'Well you'd better go home,' she said. So I did, and found Mum coming up the Wynd looking for me.

'Where **have** you been, Basil?' she said — her usual greeting those days. Jean, who had come with me just to make sure I was safe, said to her,

'Stopping all the traffic on King Street before going into the Off-Licence!'

'One thing I hate is slippery floors!'

'Oh dear,' said Mum. That was all: 'Oh dear'! Not a word of apology to me. Mind you, she was very good at saying 'sorry' except when she lost me, when she seemed to think it was my fault.

It wasn't only me she lost. She once couldn't find her car keys. She'd put them down on the oven and found them weeks later under the electric hotplate on the hob, cooked to a frazzle. I had noticed a peculiar smell but I hadn't liked to say anything.

One of Mum's failings was that she would forget to introduce me to people. One day we had gone to Auntie Lynne's and her mother was there. Mum said she would like to go to Ayr Races (that's in Scotland where I was born) and Auntie Lynne's mother offered to put me up for the night — because she came from Scotland too. Mum thanked her politely and asked, 'Is it all right if I bring Basil with me?'

Well, you should have seen Auntie Lynne's mother's face! She thought I must be a gentleman-friend that Auntie Lynne hadn't told her about! She was very broad-minded and said that it would be all right, but she looked quite relieved when she had been told who Basil was.

Chapter Twenty-One

One thing I hate is slippery floors. We once went to stay at Mum's old school, Rise Convent. Everyone was very kind, and seemed to like me, but talk about 'Rise and Shine'! Mum had a terrible time having to carry me all over the place when I refused to walk on the polished floorboards. At least at home we had wall-to-wall carpeting! We had comfy chairs too, but I wasn't allowed on them. I wasn't very pleased about this so one evening I thought up a strategy. I lay on the floor in the sitting-room, pretending to be asleep when it was time for bed; Mum, being soft-hearted, didn't want to disturb me so she let sleeping dogs lie, if you'll pardon the pun. She went to bed and left the bedroom door open so that I could come in when I woke up.

I waited a good hour until I was sure she was asleep and then I jumped on to her special armchair, prepared to settle down for a night of comfort and bliss. What a shock I had! I nearly jumped out of my skin. Suddenly there was a terrible noise and flashing light and I thought it must be the Last Judgement and I was being punished for thinking up strategies.

Mum jumped out of bed and crept to the sitting-room, as scared as I was.

'Basil!' she exclaimed. 'You've switched on the television, you naughty dog!'

Well, I didn't know there would be a late-night horror film on, did I? It was her fault anyway for leaving the remote-control on her chair. I didn't try any more strategies like that again, I can tell you.

Another thing I hate is taking medicine. Pills aren't so bad; Mum used to try to fool me by hiding the pill in a bit of ham. She used to open my mouth, pop the ham-and-pill in and then close my mouth and keep it closed until I'd swallowed. That's the trouble with having a long nose; she could get a good grip on it. I used to fool her though; I would swallow the tasty morsel of ham and let the pill fall into the side of my mouth and she would have to start all over again. She wasn't very pleased at all when I did that, so in the end I would swallow the pill to make her happy.

As I said, pills weren't so bad, because I got a few tasty morsels at the same time, but when I was put in the kitchen and the door firmly closed so that I couldn't escape I knew it was Kaoline-and-Morphine time. Mum had to give me that on a spoon, but as soon as she got the spoon near my mouth I would turn my head away and the Kaolin-and-Morphine would go all over the kitchen carpet, which didn't make her happy at all!

Eventually she would give it to me outside, so that she didn't have to wash the kitchen carpet, but she used to have to wash me instead, because I used to struggle so much when she tried to hold me with one hand and pop the spoon in my mouth with the other that the medicine would spill all over me. I looked as if I'd been to the Poodle Parlour to have white highlights put on my black hairy chest.

Chapter Twenty-Two

Dogs understand a lot more than people think. Just because I pretend sometimes not to hear when people are speaking to me, or I don't take any notice, doesn't mean that I haven't understood them. Auntie Mollie can bear me out on that. She spoke to me one day (when Mum had lost me **yet again**) and I understood perfectly.

Mum and I had been out for our usual after-breakfast amble on the Batts and along Park Wynd (walk for me meant 'amble' anyway) and I got left behind as usual. Mum was in one of her deep-in-thought moods and I was having a chin-and-tail-wag with my friends; I knew she wouldn't be pleased with me when she had to come back to fetch me but I thought I might as well be in-for-a-penny-in-for-a-pound so I stayed quite a long time. When I looked up she was nowhere to be seen, so I thought I had better go and look for her pretty quick sharp.

Well, she wasn't at home so I thought she must have gone into town to buy her 'Sporting Life'. I went to the News-Agent's but she wasn't there; it was too early for the Betting-Shop to open, or the Off-Licence, so I decided to sit outside Stabler's and wait for her to come and collect her paper. She never forgot that of course! It's not very nice to think one had to take second place to a few sheets of newsprint, but Mum once explained that we were so poor she had to get some pennies somehow. Rather muddled thinking, I thought, but then she was a teacher and everyone knows that teachers are intelligent so I supposed she knew what she was doing.

Anyway, there I was, sitting on the pavement looking this way and that to see if Mum was going to appear, when along came Auntie Mollie and saw me.

'Basil,' she said, 'your mum's been looking all over for you! She's gone that way,' pointing in the direction of home.

That was all I wanted to know. I stood up and trotted off towards King Street, remembering to stop and look both ways before crossing the road, and there she was, coming down the Wynd to look for me again!

I wagged my tail and ran to greet her and then waited for her usual 'Basil where have you been I've been looking all over for you.' This time though she was pretty relieved to see me. The next time she saw Auntie Mollie out with her two Boxers (I don't know why they are called boxers; they don't look fierce enough to me) and heard what had happened, they all had a good laugh — at my expense of course. I couldn't see what was funny; I thought I had been very intelligent.

Chapter Twenty-Three

Towards the end of our life together Mum would say to me, 'Basil, you forget that I'm getting older.' Well, the boot was on the other paw too! She seemed to forget that I was even older than she was — that I was seventy and getting to be an old man. At least I wasn't becoming odd!

Did I tell you about the time she kept going in to one of the super-markets to buy one single item and then come out with it in a huge cardboard box? She did this until she had a garage full of cardboard boxes. She said it was because a friend was moving house. I felt very embarrassed, particularly as she used to come out of the shop looking very guilty indeed.

She was always making faux pas (that's French for fawlty paws). The first time we went to Auntie Pauline's to play bridge she asked Uncle Nigel if his sister was a good tennis player. That was because she hadn't been listening properly to the conversation and hadn't **cottoned on** to the fact that he was the brother of Jo Durie, who is a very famous tennis player indeed. And she used to scold me for not listening! I was very surprised that we were invited there again, but Auntie Joan must have told them that Mum was a bit odd-but-harmless and so they were able to make allowances.

One evening she had me and all her friends settled in front of the television to watch a special programme they had asked her to video, and then she found she had recorded the wrong programme! They'd all brought their own supper too! It's a wonder she has any friends left, I can tell you.

I won't embarrass her further by telling you everything she did that was odd, but one day she did something that really took the dog biscuit. It was a good job the other lady didn't take offence or Mum's reputation in the town would really have sunk to rock-bottom. We had been in the main Post Office and Mum was holding one of the doors

open, waiting for me to follow her out (I was taking my time as usual). Whilst she was standing there holding the door open and beginning to get **impatient**, the other door from the street opened and a lady came through.

'Come on, hurry up!!' Mum said. Well, the lady looked at her in astonishment! Fortunately Mum realised just in time that the lady must have thought she had meant her — and she apologised and explained that she had been saying it to me.

Uncle Nigel had a Post Office called West End at the other side of town (the West End is a very aristocratic place to have a shop, Mum said) and sometimes we would go in there for a friendly chat. One day she went in to post a parcel and found she hadn't enough money in her purse to pay for it (Mum said we were very poor because she had to keep paying the doctor to put buckets on my head). She told Uncle Nigel that she would be back in a minute and she dragged me to the Bookie's down the road, backed a horse at long odds (whatever that means) and went back to pay for the parcel out of the winnings. Everyone thought this was very funny, but I thought it was pretty embarrassing.

Conclusion

The time came when Mum grew very worried indeed about me (she didn't know how worried I was about her!) because it was getting harder and harder for me to struggle up the stairs. She didn't know what to do about it and was becoming very anxious.

One day, however, Auntie Sue rang her up and asked if she would let me go to live with her sister, a long way away. (Mum didn't know I was listening.) Auntie Sue had known how worried Mum was and she knew too that Mum was soon going to go to Africa to stay with her family and friends, and so I would have to be without her in any case for six weeks and stay with Auntie Joan. Well, Mum asked all her friends what they thought, and they thought it would be the **best thing**. Everyone was very sad and sorry for her, and Sally told her mother that she didn't want me to go, because she would miss my companionship when she went for walks.

In the end, Mum decided to let me go. She hadn't consulted me of course, but I knew I would be going to a very good home or she wouldn't have agreed; besides, I had heard Auntie Sue tell her that I would be allowed to go on the sofa!

Mum was very unhappy to lose me and when I'd gone she missed me very much, but my new owner wrote her some letters to tell her how well I'd settled and how I'd got them just where I wanted them. At least I knew that Mum would laugh about that, because she did have a sense-of-humour even though I couldn't always share it, and at least I knew she would be relieved at not having to have any more Battle-of-Wills!

THE END

PS I've ritten this book so
that when she reads it she can
have a good laff and be
reminded of me and know that
our good relationship is still
intact, (~~ad~~ and that I havent
forgotten all the big words
I lernt from her.)
                  love from Bazil

43